Breaking Free from Inherited Family Trauma: Rewriting Your Story

Breaking Free from Inherited Family Trauma: Rewriting Your Story

Copyright © 2023 by **Monday Farouq**

TABLE OF CONTENT

Introduction

Trauma and dysfunction often run in families, passed down unconsciously from one generation to the next in recurring patterns. Many of us inherit emotional wounds, destructive behaviors, and toxic mindsets that originated long before we were born. The legacy gets encoded in our psyche and physiology, shaping who we become. We end up with tendencies, fears, insecurities, anger, addictions, and ways of coping that mirror what our parents, grandparents, and even past ancestors experienced.

This is the reality of inherited family trauma. While we cannot change what happened in previous generations, we can change how it continues to influence us. We have the power to stop intergenerational cycles and heal generational trauma.

The Hidden Burden of Dysfunctional Lineage

The scars of the past remain alive within us in many forms. They lurk below the surface as unnamed sadness, pent-up rage, debilitating anxiety, or relentless self-criticism. We carry emotional burdens that do not seem to belong to us, yet we cannot shake them.

Many grow up feeling defective, convinced that something is fundamentally wrong with them. But the true source of the pain lies hidden in secrets, betrayals, abuses, or losses from previous generations - a complex web of ancestral trauma.

We inherit these wounds not only from our parents, but from generations extending far back in time. Entire family lineages can be shaped by events from decades or centuries past. Whether you realize it or not, you are part of an intergenerational journey that began before you were born.

The tragedy is that most people suffering from inherited family trauma have no understanding of what afflicts them. They blame themselves or their parents, not realizing the roots extend much deeper. Healing requires illuminating the past and addressing historic hurts that linger unresolved through generations.

Transforming Painful Legacies

The good news is that just as trauma patterns are transmitted over generations unconsciously, it is possible to break the cycle consciously. Healing ancestral wounds allows us to rewrite ancestral scripts that keep families stuck in dysfunction.

This book provides a roadmap to transforming the painful legacies encoded in your family history. By coming to terms with the past, releasing its toxic hold, and cultivating new patterns, you can free yourself from inherited burdens.

The journey begins with understanding how trauma passes from one generation to the next. From there, you will trace your own family lineage to uncover formative traumas that still echo through generations. With deeper insight into the sources of inherited family pain, you can then begin releasing old emotional wounds, rewiring unhealthy behaviors, establishing boundaries, and forgiving.

Finally, you will discover how to transform family legacies for future generations by communicating and connecting in healthy ways, raising conscious children, and becoming the ancestor your descendants deserve.

You cannot change your ancestry, but you can change your relationship to your ancestry. The goal is not to blame those who came before, but to understand them - and through that understanding, liberate yourself. You will learn to make peace with the past, while stepping forward as author of your own life story.

Rewriting Your Story

This book provides the keys for breaking free from destructive family legacies that keep you trapped in a painful narrative. By illuminating your family system and changing how you relate to it, you can rewrite your story.

You have the power to overcome inherited burdens that have weighed you down for so long by building a conscious relationship with your ancestors. When you transform and heal generational trauma, you set an empowered example for your descendants.

The cycle can end here. Your family's destiny no longer has to be defined by its history. You have the capacity to be the ancestor who changes everything for the generations to come.

Are you ready to break free from inherited family trauma and step forward as author of your own life? This book will lead you through the journey. Let us begin.

Chapter 1: How Trauma is Passed Down

Trauma casts a long shadow, echoing across decades and generations in recurring cycles of suffering. Unhealed wounds not only haunt those directly affected, but indirectly impact their children, grandchildren, and beyond.

This phenomenon of trauma being transmitted from one generation to the next is the reality of intergenerational or inherited family trauma. In this chapter, we will explore:

- What trauma entails and its effects on individuals.

- Key mechanisms for the intergenerational transmission of trauma

- Types of inherited family trauma

- The collective nature of ancestral trauma

Armed with this understanding of how trauma passes down, you will be equipped to explore your own family history in the following chapters.

Understanding Trauma

Trauma is defined as an emotionally disturbing experience that overwhelms an individual's capacity to cope. It can stem from a single traumatic event or ongoing abuse, neglect or dysfunction.

Trauma disrupts normal development and the ability to integrate thoughts, feelings and behaviors in a healthy way. It can have profound impacts on neurological, psychological, and social functioning.

Common symptoms of unresolved trauma include:

- Hypervigilance and anxiety

- Intrusive memories or flashbacks

- Nightmares and insomnia

- Emotional dysregulation

- Depression and despair

- Anger issues

- Low self-esteem

- Difficulty maintaining relationships

- Self-harm or addiction

When faced with traumatic events, the nervous system goes into overdrive, getting stuck in survival mode long after danger has passed. This is why trauma can continue plaguing people throughout their lives without treatment.

Intergenerational Transmission

Unfortunately, the catastrophic effects of trauma do not end with the traumatized individual. Emotional and psychological scars can be passed down to children and further generations.

This happens even when descendants have no direct knowledge of the original trauma experienced by ancestors. They inherit the subconscious wounds, pain and unhealthy patterns of coping.

For example, the children of Holocaust survivors often struggle with anxiety, attachment issues, and unrealistic fears - despite never experiencing concentration camps. The trauma of the Holocaust lives on, transmitted to successive generations emotionally and biologically.

There are a number of key mechanisms for this intergenerational transmission of trauma:

Epigenetic Changes

Epigenetics is the study of how external factors alter how genes are expressed. Traumatic experiences can trigger epigenetic changes that modify how DNA functions.

Modifications do not change the DNA sequence itself but impact how genes are turned on or off. These epigenetic alterations in gene expression can enable the lasting transmission of trauma across generations.

Animal studies have demonstrated that traumatic stress alters brain structures and behaviors through epigenetic mechanisms, changes that persist in offspring. So, descendants inherit a nervous system already primed with a fear response even without lived trauma experiences.

Insecure Attachment

Early childhood attachment patterns with caregivers exert a major influence on development that persists through life. Secure attachment produces emotional resilience, while insecure attachment is linked to later psychological instability.

Trauma inhibits a caregiver's ability to form a secure attachment bond with their children. These attachment issues then interfere with the caregiver's capacity to attune to and regulate their child's nervous system and emotions.

In this way, trauma disrupts healthy attachment between generations, laying the foundation for transmission of insecure attachment styles.

Impaired Parenting

Unhealed trauma diminishes one's ability to be an effective parent, continuing cycles of dysfunction. For example, trauma survivors struggling with difficult emotions may be inconsistent, distant, abusive, or neglectful toward their own children.

Their parenting suffers because soothing and regulating their children triggers painful memories and unsettling emotions from their own past. A traumatized parent's impaired responses can inflict developmental trauma on children.

Silence and Secrecy

Trauma also lives on through silence. Many survivors are reluctant to talk about their traumatic histories. Children then grow up without understanding what happened to their parents or how it continues to haunt the family.

This powerful silence transmits trauma by blocking healing conversations that could release pain from the past. Family secrets fuel dysfunction across generations.

Maladaptive Coping Mechanisms

When faced with trauma, people adopt various coping strategies to manage distressing symptoms. However, many of these survival mechanisms are ultimately maladaptive.

An alcoholic parent self-medicates with substances. A depressed parent withdraws emotionally. An anxious parent becomes overprotective and controlling. Traumatized individuals pass down their dysfunctional attempts at coping with pain.

Without intervention, descendants mimic these unhealthy strategies, propagating them through the generations.

Collective Trauma

In addition to familial trauma, entire communities can share a traumatic history that becomes woven into collective identity. Survivors and their families may struggle with similar emotional scars:

- **Slavery** - Intergenerational trauma among African Americans rooted in the brutality of slavery and ongoing racism.

- **Genocide** - Historical mass violence and cultural erasure leaves trauma legacies affecting generations of Indigenous/Aboriginal peoples.

- **Internment Camps** - Collective trauma persists from the harsh confinement of entire ethnic groups, as with Japanese Americans in WWII.

- **Holocaust** - Not only Jewish survivors but also their children and grandchildren grapple with the generational impact.

- **Colonization** - Indigenous populations traumatized by violent colonization pass down collective wounds.

- **Apartheid** - Institutionalized oppression echoing through generations, as in South Africa.

Cultural, community-level trauma can be inherited similarly to familial trauma - through biological changes, parenting disruptions, unhealthy coping behaviors, conspiracy of silence, and pervasive despair.

Population-wide cataclysmic events filter down through the generations. Just as no one escapes individual trauma unscarred, no group escapes collective trauma unchanged. Entire lineages are imprinted with haunting legacies.

Types of Inherited Family Trauma

In your own family history, you may discover different forms of passed down trauma:

Early Loss or Abandonment

When children lose caregivers through death, deportation, imprisonment, or abandonment, it threatens emotional security lifelong. The trauma of broken attachments can echo through generations.

Physical or Sexual Abuse

Abuse inflicted by parents, relatives or family acquaintances puts children at risk for long-term psychological harm. Violence or molestation in childhood predisposes survivors to pass down trauma through impaired parenting, mental illness or addiction.

Neglect

Persistently deficient care and emotional unavailability from parents comes with devastating developmental consequences. Neglected children often internalize toxic shame and struggle bonding with their own kids.

Family Violence

Witnessing familial or parental violence, even in the absence of direct mistreatment, can result in trauma. Children in violent homes absorb fear and volatility that they may later continue in their own relationships.

Incarceration

Parental incarceration is an increasingly common source of childhood trauma with multigenerational impacts. Children of inmates face heightened risk for mental health problems, substance abuse, and entering the criminal justice system.

Family Mental Illness

Growing up with a mentally ill parent who cannot adequately care for children or regulate their emotions often results in developmental trauma. Mental illness then cycles through generations.

Addiction

Family dynamics are disrupted by parental alcoholism or substance abuse, leading to disorder, neglect, and inconsistent parenting. Genetic predispositions combine with destabilizing environments to transmit addiction across generations.

In exploring your family history for sources of inherited trauma, you may uncover many of these themes. Recognition is the critical first step in healing.

Breaking Free From Destructive Legacies

The wounds that weigh on you most heavily may not originate in your life, but in your ancestral past. Trauma leaves legacies that can endure silently through generations.

However, you have the power to break destructive cycles. By understanding how trauma passes down, facing your family history, releasing old wounds, and cultivating new patterns, you can free yourself from inherited burdens.

The next chapter examines common dynamics in dysfunctional families that perpetuate trauma across generations. Recognizing these unhealthy patterns is essential before you can rewrite them.

Healing your family lineage begins with knowing where you came from. Your ancestors' unresolved pain does not have to become your life sentence. The legacy can end here. You have the power to transform generations to come.

Chapter 2: Common Patterns in Dysfunctional Families

Trauma and dysfunction tend to run in families, recycled through recurring unhealthy patterns across generations. Destructive legacies are perpetuated not only through direct abuse but through more subtle yet damaging family dynamics.

In this chapter, we explore the most common patterns that emerge in dysfunctional families shaped by unresolved ancestral trauma:

- Denial and secrecy
- Authoritarian control
- Triangulation
- Shame and blame
- Emotional volatility
- Parentification and role reversal
- Fear-based conditioning
- Enmeshment and lack of boundaries
- Addictions and compulsive behaviors
- Emphasis on appearances

Understanding these dysfunctional family patterns is key to making sense of your own family experience. Recognizing unhealthy legacies empowers you to rewrite them.

Denial and Secrecy

"We don't talk about that in this family."

Many families buttress trauma legacies through denial and secrecy. It becomes taboo to discuss traumatic events or vulnerable emotions associated with the past. Important truths get buried.

Survivors are pressured explicitly or implicitly to keep silent and pretend everything is fine. Children grow up confused and walking on eggshells, knowing lurking issues must not be named.

This pervasive denial feeds dysfunction by blocking open conversations and healing. Trauma festers unaddressed beneath the façade. Future generations end up inheriting pain they cannot comprehend because the origins remain shrouded in secrecy.

Authoritarian Control

In response to underlying insecurity, traumatized family members often resort to excessive control in attempting to feel safe. Obedience to authority is valued over autonomy.

Rigid, authoritarian parents enforce harsh rules, demand rigid conformity, and dole out disproportionate punishments. This oppressive environment inhibits emotional expression, instills fear, and damages self-esteem.

Children must suppress their feelings and defer to domineering parents, perpetuating cycles of trauma. Scars and survival tactics get passed down through oppressive family power structures.

Triangulation

Triangulation occurs when conflict or anxiety between two family members is reduced by bringing in a third member. This shifts tension outward onto a scapegoat.

For example, if stressed parents are arguing, one may criticize or blame a child as a distraction. The child ends up carrying and reflecting stress that is not their own.

In severe cases, the family black sheep may even be ostracized and abused for failing to deflect tensions. This emotional triangulation displaces and perpetuates trauma.

Shame and Blame

Toxic shame and blame often become entrenched in traumatized families. Rather than receiving nurturance, children are made to feel inherently defective if they have needs or make mistakes.

Parents hyperfocus on flaws while neglecting strengths. Punishments far exceed crimes, communicating that the child is rotten inside. Love becomes transactional, dependent on perfect behavior.

Shaming and blaming wounds a child's spirit, instilling a sense of worthlessness. Their own children end up internalizing shame, thinking they are undeserving of love - a tragic legacy.

Emotional Volatility

Trauma breeds difficulty regulating emotions, exacerbated under stress. In volatile families, outbursts, mood swings, unpredictable behavior, and overreactions are common.

Children suffer chronic anxiety navigating their parents' emotional rollercoaster. Needs and feelings get suppressed to avoid rocking the boat. Volatile reactivity continues intergenerationally until the original trauma gets addressed.

Parentification and Role Reversal

When parents are unable or unwilling to fulfill parental duties, children are forced to fill the void. This parentification places inappropriate responsibilities on a child.

Young children may end up caring for siblings, running the household, earning money or even meeting a parent's emotional needs. Their own development gets neglected as they sacrifice childhood to accommodate the parent.

Incomplete childhoods ripple forward, as those who grew up too fast often struggle later with setting boundaries as adults or resent their children's dependence.

Fear-Based Conditioning

In traumatized families, fear often becomes the primary means of control. Instead of developing secure attachments, children are conditioned through punishment, threats, criticism, and rejection to avoid upsetting their parents.

Hypervigilance and anxiety persist, as danger always feels just around the corner. Children internalize the lesson that love is conditional on perfect behavior, breeding shame and hiding their feelings.

This fear-based conditioning serves to transmit trauma across generations unconsciously. Descendants inherit anxiety, difficulty with trust, and skewed understanding of love.

Enmeshment and Lack of Boundaries

Unclear boundaries in family relationships can enable trauma to spread pervasively across generations. When privacies are intruded upon, independence discouraged, and emotional fusion excessive, children flounder.

Enmeshed in their parents' unresolved trauma, they lack their own anchored sense of identity. Roles get confused, with children feeling excessively responsible for their parents' emotions and needs.

By adulthood, enmeshment survivors often struggle to set healthy boundaries. They transmit entangled relationships, dependence, and invasive or clinging behaviors to their own kids.

Addictions and Compulsive Behaviors

Traumatic distress often manifests through addictions and compulsions that serve as coping mechanisms. However, these problematic behaviors tend to run in families intergenerationally.

A parent's alcoholism, substance dependency, gambling addiction, excessive internet use, pornography habit, chronic overeating, or anorexia serves as a model. Genetic susceptibility combines with acquired maladaptive coping strategies.

Children absorb addiction-prone models of self-regulation rooted in escapism and compulsiveness. Without addressing the original trauma, future generations wrestle their own addictions.

Emphasis on Appearances

For some dysfunctional families shaped by trauma or abuse, maintaining perfect external appearances becomes essential. Rigid expectations around performance, manners, cleanliness, academic achievement, and societal image rule supreme.

However, the pressure to present an impeccable façade hides internal suffering, buried secrets, and strict authoritarian control behind closed doors. Children internalize the message that their intrinsic value depends on meeting the family's standards.

When appearance trumps authenticity across generations, children inherit unresolved pain masked by performance. The deeper emotional truths remain obscured by efforts to look functional.

Rewriting Dysfunctional Legacies

The good news is that by recognizing unhealthy intergenerational patterns such as these, you can rewrite them. Insight into how trauma operates in families is the first step toward growth.

If one generation can heal their ancestral traumas, they spare future generations from unconsciously repeating dysfunctional cycles. You have the power to become an ancestor who leaves a legacy of health.

The next chapter examines in more depth the impacts that unresolved ancestral trauma can exert upon descendants unconsciously afflicted by inherited family burdens.

Chapter 3: The Impact of Unresolved Trauma

Inherited family trauma leaves descendants struggling with unexplained pain, destructive behaviors, and a sense of carrying burdens not their own. When ancestral wounds go unrecognized and unhealed, they unconsciously shape lives across generations.

In this chapter, we will explore some of the most common ways unresolved ancestral trauma impacts descendants, including:

- Mental health challenges

- Relationship issues

- Low self-esteem and shame

- Physical health effects

- Dysfunctional parenting

- Maladaptive coping behaviors

- Intrusive thoughts and emotions

- Reenactment

- Fractured sense of self

- Spiritual disconnection

Understanding these resonating effects empowers us to break free from generational trauma.

Mental Health Challenges

Unresolved trauma exponentially increases one's risk for mental health issues such as anxiety, depression, PTSD, and substance abuse. When passed down, it puts descendants at similar risk, even without directly experiencing the inciting traumatic events.

Living with inherited fear, pain, and unhealthy coping behaviors breeds psychological distress. The brain and nervous system carry imprints of ancestral trauma that manifest through disorders. Epigenetic changes increase vulnerabilities.

Seeking mental health support provides tools to cope, but addressing inherited family trauma is key to unlocking the roots of dysfunction. Healing intergenerational wounds prevents perpetuating them.

Relationship Issues

Early attachment trauma fuels challenges with relationships and intimacy throughout life. When parents cannot attune to children's needs due to their own unhealed wounds, it derails healthy attachment.

This gets passed down as descendants struggle to trust partners, set boundaries, communicate openly, navigate conflict, and tolerate vulnerability. Unconscious relationship patterns echo through generations.

Doing your own work to heal ancestral trauma can help you break destructive relational legacies. The past does not have to define your future relationships.

Low Self-Esteem and Toxic Shame

Inherited trauma breeds toxic shame and chronically low self-esteem. Children internalize the message of being unwanted, unlovable, defective, unimportant, or worthless.

Growing up with parents who are inconsistent, abusive, or neglectful due to their trauma warps one's self-perception. Shame and lack of self-worth get transmitted unconsciously.

Recognizing these core wounds as ancestral heirlooms rather than personal truths is hugely empowering. You can begin releasing distorted self-perceptions by healing generational trauma.

Physical Health Effects

Unresolved trauma impacts the body profoundly, compromising long-term health. Chronic hyperarousal of the nervous system wears down physiological systems.

Stress hormones like cortisol and adrenaline, useful short-term, become toxic long-term. Immune function is impaired. Inflammation increases. Reproductive, digestive, cardiovascular, and neuroendocrine systems get off-kilter.

These bodily effects of trauma get woven into descendants' health when not addressed. Healing trauma has been proven to improve overall wellbeing.

Dysfunctional Parenting

Parents unknowingly transmit the harm they've experienced, perpetuating cycles of trauma with the adage, "Those who are hurt end up hurting others."

Unhealed trauma undermines patience, presence, emotional attunement, consistency, communication, and healthy bonding with children. Generational wounds keep getting passed down through dysfunctional parenting.

However, you can choose to disrupt the cycle with your own children by healing your ancestral traumas first. Parenting with present mind, empathy, and emotional intelligence prevents further transmission.

Maladaptive Coping Behaviors

Unhealthy coping mechanisms develop to manage intolerable trauma-based emotions and symptoms. These survival adaptations include addictions, eating disorders, perfectionism, people-pleasing, zoning out, self-harm, aggression, dissociation, and more.

When passed down through generations, descendants reflexively resort to the same maladaptive strategies, even without the context of the precipitating trauma. Breaking free requires undoing survival programming.

Intrusive Thoughts and Emotions

Inherited family trauma haunts unconsciously through invasive thoughts, emotions, dreams, and body sensations that don't feel fully your own. They get projected internally in fragmented ways.

Negative self-talk echoing ancestors' voices. Dread attached to no current threat. Inexplicable rage, panic, grief, or pain. Symptoms baffling until one understands their generational source.

Connecting to lineages allows us to externalize inherited inner experiences rather than pathologizing ourselves as defective.

Reenactment

The unconscious mind's attempt to resolve past trauma causes people to reenact it through cycles of repeating destructive choices. We recreate what we cannot release.

Children who suffer abuse from an alcoholic parent may develop a later desire for intoxication. Someone abandoned reenacts heartbreak through serial cheating. Without ending the transmission, descendants relive ancestral traumas.

Awareness is key to diverging from tragic scripts. By engaging in your own healing process, you refuse unconscious reenactment.

Fractured Sense of Self

Trauma fractures the psyche and disrupts identity formation. When caregiving relationships needed for secure attachment are tenuous and unreliable due to ancestral trauma, children lack foundations from which to develop a cohesive sense of self.

Without past wounds being seen, named, and grieved, descendants float through life disconnected from their histories. Healing your lineage is key to feeling whole.

Spiritual Disconnection

Unresolved trauma often severs people's connection to meaning, purpose, faith, and the sacred. When trust is profoundly ruptured or the world ceases to make sense, trauma challenges previous belief systems.

This spiritual estrangement or lack of grounding in something larger than oneself also passes down through generations unconsciously. Restoring spiritual connection emerges from healing.

Rewriting Your Story

The ways unhealed ancestral trauma shapes lives are complex and pervasive. However, insight into these resonating impacts empowers us to rewrite generational stories.

Your patterns, behaviors and struggles are not dysfunctional character flaws to be ashamed of. They are echoes of your ancestors' unresolved pain.

By beginning the intergenerational healing process, you can break unhealthy cycles. The next chapters provide a roadmap to freeing yourself from inherited burdens so that you may live in alignment with your true potential.

Chapter 4: Tracing Your Family History

Exploring your family history and ancestral lineages is a pivotal part of the intergenerational trauma healing process. Uncovering past traumas, losses, secrets, and dysfunctional patterns provides critical missing context for your struggles.

In this chapter, we will discuss:

- Why learning your family history matters

- How to trace your family lineage

- Gathering family histories and stories

- Identifying key traumatic events and recurring themes

- Processing difficult emotions that arise

- Using genograms to map family systems

- Releasing guilt and moving forward

By tracing your lineages and discovering ancestral roots, you honor those who came before while freeing future generations.

Why Your Family History Matters

Tracing your family history illuminates the inherited traumas, challenges, secrets, addictions, and dysfunctions that helped shape who you are today in ways you may never have realized.

Seeing how past generations responded to the circumstances they faced with the tools they had provides understanding, forgiveness, and critically, context. It allows you to externalize what you absorbed unconsciously.

Knowing your ancestral stories allows you to discern which feelings, fears, patterns, inner critic voices, somatic symptoms, and beliefs originated with you vs. were transmitted intergenerationally. This knowledge is profoundly liberating.

Your family history explains how you arrived here - and where to focus healing.

How to Trace Your Lineage

Tracing your family lineage takes curiosity, an open heart, and a bit of detective work. Here are some tips:

Talk to close family members - Have in-depth conversations with parents, grandparents, aunts, uncles, and other relatives to learn about past generations. Ask about their childhoods, traumas, the relatives they knew, family stories passed down, any secrets revealed. Listen for recurring themes.

Look through family photographs and documents - Peruse old letters, journals, bibles, certificates, scrapbooks, immigration paperwork, and albums for clues into your ancestors' lives. Make notes about what you discover.

Do genealogical research online - Sites like Ancestry.com allow you to search records to trace family trees and locate information about your ancestors. U.S. census data, immigration paperwork, marriage/death certificates, and obituaries can provide insights.

Visit ancestral places - Travel to where your ancestors lived, if possible. Walking in their footsteps, seeing old homes, gravesites, villages or tribal lands can help you feel connected to relatives from the past and imagine what shaped them.

Pull at heartstrings - Allow yourself to get emotional as you investigate your family history. Pay attention to when you feel unexpectedly sad, angry, anxious, or moved. Your body may offer clues toward ancestral wounds.

Follow your intuition as you unravel family lineages. Let the process of discovery unfold.

Gathering Family Stories

Collecting oral histories from your living relatives preserves family stories that provide windows into generational patterns, traumas, secrets, and soul gifts.

Ask probing questions and follow threads as stories emerge. Record conversations to revisit revelations you may have missed. Treat family members as the experts on the history held in their bodies.

Open-ended questions to ask relatives might include:

- What was your childhood like?

- What do you know about your grandparents/great-grandparents?

- What stories do you remember your relatives telling you when you were young?

- What struggles did family members face?

- Were there any family secrets?

- Are there patterns you noticed getting repeated in the family?

- What brought your ancestors to this area or country?

- What values/traditions have been passed down in the family?

- What health conditions or illnesses often affect your family members?

- How did your family handle difficult emotions like anger or sadness?

Thank relatives for their generosity in sharing family histories. Cherishing ancestral stories is a legacy itself.

Identifying Traumatic Events

As you gather family histories, make note of traumatic events, dramatic turning points, and sources of generational pain for your family. Some examples:

- War, genocide, colonization, slavery, forced relocation

- Loss of family members or homeland/displacement through immigration

- Extreme poverty, forced labor, lack of opportunities

- Family mental illness, suicide or substance addiction

- Physical/sexual abuse, emotional neglect, domestic violence

- Secret out-of-wedlock births, children given up

- Incarceration, institutionalization, or criminal activity

- Disownment or family estrangement

Look for common themes such as abandonment, severe deprivation, betrayal, cultural oppression, death/illness, or violation of bodily sovereignty. Mark events that shattered family trust.

Processing Difficult Emotions

Uncovering your family's past traumas can stir up intense feelings as you empathetically connect to ancestral pain. Profound grief, rage, anxiety, despair may arise. You may feel the vulnerabilities and staggering losses of those before you.

Allow yourself to feel without drowning in emotions. Bear witness to the heartbreaking histories. Get support and practice self-care when flooded by painful revelations. This is part of releasing old burdens - by feeling them fully first.

Using Genograms to Map Your Family

Creating a genogram can help you map family relationships and see intergenerational patterns visually. Genograms are diagrams that depict multigenerational connections between family members, major events, and trends over time.

Genograms include symbols such as:

- Circles and squares to represent female/male relatives

- Lines between figures depicting relationships

- Dates of births, deaths, marriages, divorces

- Emotional closeness or conflict between relatives

- Recurring situations such as addiction, mistreatment, and mental health issues.

Studying your family genogram illuminates influential patterns passed through lineages unconsciously. You gain perspective on how you arrived where you are as part of an ancestral web.

Releasing Guilt

In the process of tracing family histories, you may feel a sense of guilt or responsibility when you uncover patterns of mistakes, wrongs, or "sins" committed across generations.

"If my great-grandfather hadn't abandoned the family, my grandfather wouldn't have become an alcoholic..." The impulse is to fantasize how you could have changed things for the better.

However, remember the choices of your ancestors are not your burdens to carry. Their traumas and coping mechanisms made sense given what they faced and the limitations of their times. You cannot rewrite the past. Your gift is learning from it in order to heal the future.

The next chapter guides you in identifying how your ancestors' unresolved wounds echo in your life today so that you may continue the healing journey.

Chapter 5: Connecting the Dots - How the Past Affects You

With knowledge of your ancestral histories and inherited family traumas, you can begin connecting the dots to how the past unconsciously affects your life today. This chapter explores:

- Recognizing generational PTSD

- How to reflect on your patterns and struggles

- Identifying echoes of ancestral traumas

- Exploring your emotional triggers

- Using journaling and inner child work

- Talking to family about intergenerational cycles

- Being gentle with yourself

- Honoring your ancestors' resilience

Illuminating the threads between your ancestors' unresolved wounds and your inner world allows you to break free from the past.

Recognizing Generational PTSD

Unresolved ancestral trauma often manifests in descendants as a form of generational PTSD - post-traumatic stress disorder.

While you may not have experienced your ancestors' original inciting traumas firsthand, the legacy lives on in your nervous system, psychology, and behaviors. Their trauma shaped your developmental environment, relationships, and attachment patterns early on.

Generational PTSD can take the form of:

- Hypervigilance and anxiety

- Depression, dread, or emotional numbness

- Insomnia, panic attacks, nightmares

- Cognitive difficulties like poor memory or confusion

- Emotional dysregulation and reactivity

- Addictions and compulsive habits

- Somatic symptoms like digestion issues, body pain, breathing difficulties

Start recognizing how your ancestors' traumas left you with a legacy of PTSD symptoms. Generational healing begins with awareness.

Reflecting on Your Patterns

Begin reflecting on how your family history and inherited traumas may have unconsciously shaped tendencies and behaviors you struggle with:

- Perfectionism

- People-pleasing

- Difficulty trusting others

- Need for control

- Harsh self-judgment

- Fear of conflict

- Feeling perpetually unsafe

- Addiction prone

- Difficulty with intimacy

- Escapism behaviors

- Self-sabotage

Inquire within, pondering, "Considering the circumstances our ancestors confronted, how could this pattern have been advantageous?" Recognizing your actions as inheritances rather than individual deficiencies can kindle empathy for both yourself and your family.

Identifying Ancestral Echoes

Beyond patterns, start paying attention to ways you experience emotional echoes of your ancestors' unresolved pain.

Do you carry inexplicable grief, despair, or loneliness? Feel self-loathing? Carry free-floating anxiety? Struggle with nameless rage? Have irrational vigilant fear? Suffer without identifiable cause?

Explore if these could be signals from past generations asking you to help lay their burdens down at last. Their traumas instinctively got funneled into you awaiting release.

Exploring Your Triggers

Notice what experiences, words, situations, places, smells, or even names unexpectedly trigger intense distress, panic, dread, rage, or sadness in you.

Triggers reveal your nervous system's sensitivity around ancestral wounds. Explore if certain triggers relate directly to traumas your family endured historically.

Deep in our bodies, we carry the memories of our lineage. Lean into any painful triggers as guides toward ancestral healing work.

Using Journaling and Inner Child Work

Journaling allows you to access intuitive insights about ancestry and intergenerational trauma through stream of consciousness writing.

Try closing your eyes, getting grounded in your body, and asking inwardly, "How do my ancestors' traumas affect me?" Keep writing your responses without self-judgment.

Additionally, try inner child work by dialoguing journal-style with your wounded inner child self. Ask them, "What ancestral burdens do you carry?" Stay open to messages from your deeper self.

Talking with Family

Once you have reflected personally, have vulnerable discussions with family members about ancestral trauma impacting you collectively across generations.

Ask if they perceive similar echoes from the past in themselves and your family dynamics. When connections surface through dialogue, hidden wisdom gets unveiled.

Creating a safe container for kind-hearted family truth-telling fosters communal ancestral healing. You are all walking each other home.

Being Gentle with Yourself

Remember to be exceedingly gentle with yourself as you unpack generational trauma. There may be pain, anger, or shame as your psyche unearths repressed memories from the past. Your body may need extra nurturing.

Practice meeting any emotions with compassion and patience rather than criticism. This healing journey takes time, courage, and profound self-love. Celebrate each step.

Honoring Ancestral Resilience

While examining painful family histories, also make sure to acknowledge the remarkable resilience of your ancestors who survived despite trauma and adversity.

The fact that you are here today is testament to their grit, faith, courage, and perseverance. Your existence is their victory. Holding reverence for those before you keeps learning ancestry's lessons balanced.

Gaining insight into how the past unconsciously affects you empowers your healing journey ahead. The next chapter delves into strategies for facing family secrets and breaking harmful silence.

Chapter 6: Breaking the Silence - Facing Family Secrets

Family secrets fuel the transmission of intergenerational trauma by burying painful truths in shadows. Shedding light on secrets through open communication promotes healing across generations.

This chapter explores:

- The damaging effects of family secrets

- Types of hidden truths

- Ways secrets get perpetuated

- Why silence is not the answer

- Having courageous conversations

- Handling family members' resistance

- Getting support for disclosure

- Forgiving betrayals of trust

- Learning to integrate revelations

Breaking family silence removes barriers to healing, while bringing understanding and connection.

The Damaging Effects of Secrets

Family secrets exert toxic effects, both individually and collectively across generations. Secrets breed:

- Shame and guilt

- Anxiety from perpetual threat of exposure

- Identity confusion

- Undermined sense of belonging

- Distrust within family relationships

- Interpersonal dysfunction

- Lack of emotional authenticity/vulnerability

- Enabling of continuing abuse/addiction

At the same time, secrecy blocks open communication needed for healing and intimacy. Emotional repression required to maintain silence becomes intergenerational trauma in itself.

Types of Hidden Truths

Some examples of painful truths frequently kept hidden in families include:

Abuse - Physical, verbal, emotional, or sexual abuse by family members may remain unspoken. Victims are shamed into silence.

Addiction - Alcoholism, drug abuse, gambling compulsions, or other addictions often occur covertly, denied by family members.

Mental illness - Histories of psychiatric disorders, hospitalizations, depression, anxiety, suicide attempts, etc. may be swept under the rug.

Physical/developmental disabilities - Disabilities, both visible or invisible, get ignored rather than discussed compassionately.

Criminal activity - Relatives' involvement in crime, jail time, unethical deeds, or legal transgressions may be considered taboo.

Hidden medical diagnoses - Health conditions like HIV, cancer, neurological disorders, or genetic diseases can be treated as embarrassing secrets.

Family estrangements - Rifts, falling-outs, and relationship breakdowns often happen quietly, leaving confusion in their wake.

Adoptions - Closed adoptions and unknown parentage are frequently hushed. Adoptees struggle with fractured identity.

Conceptions out of wedlock - Stigma and "illegitimacy" cloaked details of unplanned pregnancies and youthful affairs.

Financial circumstances - Money issues like family wealth/poverty, bankruptcy, debt, inheritable assets, and social class may be obscured.

Ancestry - Racial or ethnic identity, immigration status, cultural heritage, and even last names may be masked to avoid discrimination.

Non-mainstream sexual/gender identities - Due to prejudice, belonging to LGBTQIA+ communities stays unspoken and invalidated.

Any truth that disrupts the façade of a perfect, functional family risks getting minimized and denied.

How Secrets Get Perpetuated

Generational family silence gets maintained through overt and subtle means:

- Victims being shamed, guilted, or threatened into keeping abuse secret

- Social taboos that prevent discussing topics like mental illness or sexuality

- Lies told to cover embarrassing or "disgraceful" events

- Unstated rules against expressing vulnerable emotions

- Avoiding difficult conversations to keep up appearances

- Controlling family members dominating narratives and silencing dissent

- Scapegoating those who try exposing truths

- Pretending problems like addiction do not exist

- Hiding archival records that reveal less favorable histories

Questioning collusive secrets threatens the "respectable family" illusion. A legacy of silence serves to bury traumatic realities.

Why Silence is Not the Answer

Many avoid revealing family secrets because they believe speaking painful truths will damage the family. However, the opposite is true - secrecy is what erodes family foundations.

Hiding trauma and dysfunction enables unhealthy patterns to persist unchecked. Only by shining a compassionate light of awareness on dark events and emotions can healing begin.

While exposing secrets is challenging in the short-term, honest engagement with the past fosters intimacy and trust over the long-term. Wholeness depends on truth.

Having Courageous Conversations

Start facing painful family secrets by having caring one-on-one conversations with both older and younger generations in your family.

Communicate your desire to foster healing together by discussing issues openly. Emphasize concern for their wellbeing and better understanding one another, not judgment.

Ask how they feel about breaking generational silence. Assure them that acknowledging past wounds will strengthen, not destroy, family bonds. Remain patient and non-reactive. This may be the beginning of an ongoing dialogue.

Handling Family Resistance

You may encounter defensiveness when trying to discuss uncomfortable family secrets. Your motives, character, or sanity may get questioned.

Remember, their resistance likely stems from shame or wanting to maintain status quo, not because you are wrong to seek truth. Breathe through distrust. Your courage plants seeds even if they do not immediately see it.

Offer empathy for their need to feel safe. Explain why you feel healing will come from openness. Remind them that with silence, trauma repeats - with honesty, it can end.

Getting Support for Disclosure

Revealing or discussing family secrets you have uncovered can stir many emotions - anxiety, anger, dread, confusion, heartbreak. You may feel alone or need guidance.

Reach out to a trusted therapist or counselor experienced with intergenerational trauma. Join a support group. The relief of being heard and validated can strengthen you enormously. You deserve backing.

Forgiving Betrayals of Trust

Realizing trusted relatives betrayed you or lied by omission through maintaining generational secrets can provoke justifiable anger and feelings of betrayal.

Work on forgiving family members who failed you by hiding difficult truths or pressuring your silence. They likely acted to survive trauma themselves, not maliciously. Beneath the hurt, find understanding.

Learning to Integrate Revelations

As you uncover once-hidden truths about your family history and ancestry, allow time to integrate this new information into your identity and relationships.

Facts alone do not provide meaning - do the inner work of making sense of revelations in light of your family's contexts and humanity. Ancestral healing involves weaving truths into your story with compassion.

Breaking generational silence is a risk that leads to emotional freedom from the past's burdens. You reclaim voice and power silenced in those before you. Future generations depend on your courage to speak.

The next chapter explores strategies to begin releasing old trauma stored in your body and psyche through accessing feelings, grief, and forgiveness.

Chapter 7: Releasing Emotional Pain

With awareness of your ancestral traumas, you can now begin the healing process of releasing old emotional wounds carried in your body, psyche, and nervous system across generations.

This chapter explores:

- Why past pain needs to be felt in order to heal

- Allowing yourself to grieve ancestral losses

- Identifying suppressed emotions

- Embodied practices to process feelings

- Working with anger constructively

- Exploring the ancestral source of your inner critic

- Self-compassion to transform shame

- Emotional healing as a journey

- Forgiveness as liberation

By opening up to feel the repressed hurts of your lineage consciously, you free their grip on you unconsciously.

Why Past Pain Needs to be Felt

Many attempt to outrun ancestral pain through distraction, addiction, busyness, or denial. However, the only way out is through. Frozen trauma must be unfrozen.

Trying to prematurely "get over it" or detach from intergenerational wounds without allowing full expression of the emotions keeps them lodged within.

Grieving and feeling brings release. By providing your ancestors' repressed feelings a voice at last, they find peace through you.

Allowing Yourself to Grieve

Make space to grieve ancestral losses that you carry - deaths of family in disaster, war, or genocide; loss of homeland; children given up; abandonment; betrayal of abuse; stolen dignity, culture or freedom.

Grieving is an act of love. Your tears thaw your ancestors' frozen cries. Through your willingness to mourn, their spirits are finally witnessed and able to rest.

Identifying Suppressed Emotions

Notice which emotions you struggle to express, like anger or sadness. Traced backward, these may reveal your ancestors' repressed feelings.

Your fear of appearing weak by crying may actually be centuries of forbearers forced to "get over it quickly and move on." Ancestors depending on you to break the cycle of stoicism.

Embodied Practices to Process Feelings

Physical practices help unlock suppressed emotions stored cellularly:

- Spend time vocalizing - yelling, screaming, humming, toning, singing to free emotional flow.

- Use movement - dance, shake, run, stretch to open energy systems and clear trauma physically.

- Create art to express family stories, losses and secrets too painful for words.

- Spend reflective time in nature allowing feelings to surface and move through you.

- Receive bodywork like massage, acupuncture, or reiki to open places where grief gets "stuck."

- Take cleansing baths or showers imagining washing off ancestral burdens.

Your body knows the way back home to wholeness. Follow its lead.

Working with Anger Constructively

Ancestral healing often brings up anger we carry on behalf of mistreated forbearers unable to feel safe expressing outrage over violation of dignity and rights.

Constructively channel righteous anger into activism, truth-telling, creating social change, or protecting others from harm. Your ancestors' fury longs for expression as justice.

Exploring the Roots of Your Inner Critic

That nagging "inner critic" judging your every move may actually echo ancestral voices unconsciously internalized.

Your "critical parent" often perpetuates family patterns of perfectionism, people-pleasing, performance pressure or chronic feeling "not good enough."

See if you can discern whose expectations shape your inner critic. Talk back, set boundaries, channel compassion. Healing your inner voice heals your lineage.

Using Self-Compassion to Transform Shame

Toxic shame often gets transmitted intergenerationally when trauma survivors see themselves as irreparably damaged or unlovable.

Gently confront shame by cultivating self-compassion. Address yourself with the same tenderness and care as you would a cherished child. Treat yourself with the kindness your ancestors deserved.

Affirm you are worthy not because of what you accomplish but simply because you exist. You are the living amends to your ancestors for the love they were denied.

Emotional Healing As a Journey

Remember releasing ancestral pain is a journey, not destination. Repressed feelings surface in stages when you create safety to experience them.

There will be better days when you feel lighter and more empowered, and difficult days when you feel pulled downward again by legacy burdens. Both are progress.

Keep affirming your commitment to emotional freedom. Stay patient and trust your innate healing intelligence to guide your process.

Forgiveness As Liberation

Forgiving ancestral betrayals or abuses is challenging but critical. Forgiveness is not condoning actions; it is releasing trapped energy you carry from the past.

Forgiveness loosens trauma's grip and promotes understanding. You absolve ancestral failings by acknowledging the broader context that shaped their choices and limitations.

Compassion for ancestors' humanity and suffering allows us to break free from cycles of blame into wholeness.

By bravely diving into the depths of your familial emotional pain, you resurrect repressed parts of yourself and your ancestors. Feeling is the antidote to intergenerational trauma. Your vulnerability transforms generational history.

The following chapter provides strategies to rewire patterns of thoughts, behaviors, and unconscious habits formed in response to inherited trauma. Ending ancestral cycles requires reprogramming the mind and body holistically.

Chapter 8: Rewiring Unhealthy Behavioral Patterns

Now that you have begun releasing old emotional wounds inherited from your ancestors, the next step is unraveling the unhealthy thoughts, behaviors, and coping mechanisms encoded in you by generational trauma.

This chapter explores:

- How trauma shapes neural pathways

- Identifying automatic reactions

- Rewiring fear-based patterns

- Transforming addiction legacies

- Shifting perfectionistic tendencies

- Ending cycles of abuse

- Embracing vulnerability over shame

- Letting go of limiting beliefs

- Restoring healthy boundaries

- Practicing body mindfulness

- Patience with the process

Rewiring trauma-based patterns requires reprogramming your body and mind toward safety and wholeness.

How Trauma Shapes Neural Pathways

Trauma gets encoded in implicit memory unlike explicit autobiographical memories. Implicit trauma is stored somatically through automatic fear reactions versus narrative recollection.

When faced with overwhelm, the brain goes into fight-flight-freeze survival mode, bypassing higher logic centers. Chronic stress and trauma carve neural grooves of habitual fear responses.

Healing trauma involves consciously rewiring fear-based neural pathways grooved by adversity to remap automatic reactions.

Identifying Automatic Reactions

Start by noticing patterns of thoughts, emotions or behaviors that activate automatically in situations before you have time to consciously choose how to respond.

For instance, a casual touch may evoke instant disgust. A minor criticism can trigger full shame spiral. Even small anxieties detonate into panic attacks.

Mapping your go-to stress reactions allows you to mindfully pause and choose healthier responses that break detrimental habit loops.

Rewiring Fear-Based Patterns

Trauma fuels rigid cognitive patterns like:

- Hypervigilance and paranoia

- Worst case scenario thinking

- Perceiving threats everywhere

- Harsh self-judgment

- Feeling perpetually unsafe

- Black and white thinking

When fear-based thought loops get triggered, pause and redirect your mind toward gratitude, hope, self-compassion or growth-oriented possibilities.

Replace limiting thought patterns with life-giving truths. Your mind will rewire as you practice.

Transforming Addiction Legacies

Those struggling with addictions like alcoholism, drugs, sex/porn, gambling, or food inherited susceptibility from ancestors who coped through addiction cycles.

Healing your lineage involves consciously choosing to interrupt addiction loops when they get triggered. Pause unhealthy cravings to sit with underlying feelings fueling them.

Access support like 12-step groups, counseling, meditation and healthy community that can help anchor you as you rewire addictive patterns.

Shifting Perfectionistic Tendencies

The need to be perfect often conceals a deep fear of being imperfect and unlovable. Perfectionism attempts to avoid shame, criticism, or rejection through unattainable standards.

To transform perfectionism, practice self-acceptance even when you misstep. Replace self-criticism with self-compassion. Let go of trying to control others' approval. Allow yourself to be human.

Ending Cycles of Abuse

Those who experienced or witnessed family abuse and volatility struggle with anger issues or abusive tendencies themselves. Breaking the legacy means relating to others and yourself with kindness.

Develop mindfulness skills to halt reactive anger and access deeper wisdom. Release shame by accepting responsibility and making amends for missteps. Choose peacefulness.

Embracing Vulnerability Over Shame

Generational trauma often breeds excessive sensitivity to shame and fear of vulnerability. Learning to be vulnerable despite fears of unworthiness or rejection is profoundly healing.

Take small risks to share authentically, ask for help, admit mistakes, navigate discomfort. Affirm your worthiness of belonging, love and imperfection.

Letting Go of Limiting Beliefs

Growing up with inherited family trauma can instill limiting beliefs like:

- I am undeserving

- I'll never be good enough

- I'm permanently damaged

- I don't belong anywhere

- I'll always be alone

- The world isn't safe

Confront these core wounds with loving truth and evidence that you are capable, worthy, resilient and fundamentally whole. Limiting beliefs lose power once exposed to light.

Restoring Healthy Boundaries

Generational enmeshment and dysfunction impairs ability to set healthy relational boundaries. Restore boundaries by honoring your own needs.

Practice saying no without guilt. Speak up about discomfort. Release over-responsibility for others' emotions or issues. Maintain privacy and time for yourself. Boundaries foster secure identity and intimacy.

Practicing Body Mindfulness

Trauma dysregulates the nervous system, causing mind and body to feel disconnected. Developing body mindfulness - tuning into physical sensations, emotions, and needs - heals alienation.

Try yoga, body scans, walking meditation, and other practices that gently return awareness inward. Listen to innate wisdom.

Patience with the Process

Rewiring unconscious patterns resulting from inherited trauma takes time, self-compassion, and trial-and-error. Old neural pathways will stubbornly persist out of habit.

With loving persistence and community support, new pathways are carved. Have faith in your innate resilience. You are undoing generations of hurt - be proud of each step.

As you cultivate healthier responses, you reprogram family lineages to release inherited burdens. Your ancestors and future generations are rooting for you.

The next chapter explores practices for soothing anxiety, cultivating inner peace, and anchoring yourself in a sense of safety and belonging.

Chapter 9: Cultivating Self-Compassion and Inner Peace

Inherited family trauma often leaves us carrying latent anxiety, feelings of disconnectedness, and a shaky sense of self. Learning to anchor in self-compassion and inner peace becomes integral for healing.

This chapter explores practices for:

- Developing a compassionate inner voice

- Mindfulness to ease anxiety

- Soothing nervous system dysregulation

- Inner child work to reparent yourself

- Embodying self-love and acceptance

- Finding emotional shelter in nature

- Spiritual connection for comfort

- Healthy bonding and community

- Looking inward for security

- Allowing joy and pleasure

By nurturing presence and stillness within, you transform intergenerational wounds.

Developing a Compassionate Inner Voice

Unhealthy self-talk echoing from ancestral criticism or shame is pervasive with inherited trauma. Shift your inner voice toward unconditional compassion.

Imagine speaking gently to a beloved child when you make a mistake, feel insecure, or get triggered. Allow self-kindness to quiet harsh judgment. You are safe and worthy.

Mindfulness to Ease Anxiety

Trauma breeds chronic anxiety and panic handed down through generations. Developing mindfulness allows you to release fear-based thoughts by grounding in the present moment.

Practice mindful breathing, yoga, being in nature, or activities that require full sensory attention like knitting or gardening. Mindfulness returns you to your empowered adult self.

Soothing Nervous System Dysregulation

Ancestral trauma dysregulates the nervous system, causing mental fog, emotional volatility, and physical symptoms. Soothing your nervous system restores stability.

Try calming practices like conscious breathing, vagus nerve exercises, cold water immersion, eye gazing, massage, Biofeedback, EMDR, acupuncture, chanting or prayer. Find what resonates most.

Inner Child Work to Reparent Yourself

Reconnect with your wounded inner child who carries inherited trauma and neglected needs. Envision hugging, comforting and reassuring your younger self.

Dialogue journal-style with your inner child. Validate their feelings and provide the safe holding space your ancestors could not. You can heal your own childhood.

Embodying Self-Love and Acceptance

Trauma breeds toxic shame and self-loathing. Healing involves mindfully shifting to words, actions and touch that affirm your lovability and worth.

Look at yourself in the mirror and state positive truths aloud about your value. Place hands on heart and abdomen in soothing physical connection. Massage tension from your body.

Finding Emotional Shelter in Nature

Nature's tranquility has unparalleled power to instill calm and security when anxiety persists from generational trauma.

Spend time daily sitting under a tree, walking by water, laying on the earth, or hugging a plant. Let nature's rhythms harmonize your nervous system.

Spiritual Connection for Comfort

Shared ancestral trauma often severs connection to the sacred. Seek comfort in spiritual community and practices that resonate with your values - meditation, yoga, religious services, art, community service, ceremony.

Spiritual connection awakens innate inner peace. There is a song waiting to sing you home.

Healthy Bonding and Community

Secure attachment and belonging counteract inherited attachment wounds and isolation. Prioritize relationships that allow you to feel seen, accepted, heard, and nurtured through intimacy and mutual care.

Join support groups. Volunteer. Contribute meaningfully. You deserve to feel connected.

Looking Inward for Security

Break patterns of excessively relying on others for safety, stability, and emotional regulation. Develop the secure inner base needed to trust yourself and access inner wisdom.

Sit comfortably with eyes closed and envision your core self - an infinite well of strength, compassion, and resilience unchanged by trauma. You are already whole.

Allowing Joy and Pleasure

A side-effect of inherited trauma can be disconnection from joy. Healing involves opening again to life's beauty, creativity, excitement, wonder, laughter, pleasure and childlike play.

Make time for lightness. Try new forms of artistic expression, be silly, spend time with children, move your body to music. You deserve delight.

Though the journey of reconciling generational trauma is often painful, make sure it remains bookended by self-care, safety, and nourishment. Your freedom springs eternally from within. You can rest in stillness anytime - all you must do is remember.

The following chapter explores how establishing healthy boundaries empowers you to step forward as authority in your own life story and legacy.

Chapter 10: Setting Boundaries and Letting Go

When embroiled in the dynamics of intergenerational trauma, creating healthy boundaries becomes essential for your healing journey ahead.

This chapter explores practices for:

- Understanding the role of boundaries

- Identifying your boundary needs

- Setting physical and emotional boundaries

- Managing external expectations

- Coping with guilt and pushback

- Learning to say no

- Protecting your energy

- Prioritizing self-care

- Establishing safe family interactions

- Letting go with love

- Honoring your wholeness

Setting boundaries allows you to step forward as author of your own empowered identity, separate from inherited stories and legacies passed down.

The Role of Boundaries

Boundaries create a sense of self-ownership, autonomy, and choice in how you relate to family members and situations. They regulate emotional intimacy.

Generational trauma often breeds enmeshment, dependence, confusion or invasion of role boundaries, leaving descendants feeling powerless. Reclaiming personal authority to make self-protective choices interrupts trauma dynamics.

You honor both yourself and relatives by establishing mutually compassionate limits that foster security and belonging for all.

Identifying Your Boundary Needs

Reflect on your boundary needs in areas like:

- Physical space and privacy

- Emotional distance when overwhelmed

- Time alone to recharge

- Keeping some personal details private

- Asking not to be touched or startled

- Choosing preferred topics of conversation

- Setting tech boundaries on calls, texts, social media

- Limiting demands on your time or support

- Respecting parenting decisions and house rules

Listen to your body, mind and spirit. Where do you feel invasive pressure? What causes you to shut down? Healthy boundaries reflect your soul and story - not just what others want.

Setting Physical and Emotional Boundaries

Start simply practicing respecting your own boundaries physically and emotionally.

- Ask loved ones for hugs or physical touch only when you want them

- Share feelings or details of your life only when you feel comfortable

- Leave conversations that feel overwhelming or inappropriate

- Turn off devices and spend time alone to reconnect inwardly

- Limit time spent in drama, conflict or crisis mode when needed for self-care

Small steps practicing autonomy and self-care will build confidence to navigate more complex boundary dynamics.

Managing External Expectations

Well-meaning family may unconsciously burden you with inappropriate responsibilities, needs, or emotions due to blurred boundaries. Manage demands wisely.

- Gently refuse requests that cause you resentment or drain your energy. Don't sacrifice your well-being to provide comfort to others.

- Challenge expectations to always be cheerful and compliant when you need authenticity.

- Take space from energy-draining relatives without guilt when required for your health.

Your worth and rights do not decrease because others need help. Empowerment means meeting your own needs first.

Coping With Guilt and Pushback

Establishing healthier boundaries naturally provokes pushback from family used to controlling you or offloading their burdens onto you. Stay strong.

When relatives guilt or shame you, remember:

- You are not responsible for their emotions or issues

- Adulthood means relating to parents as equals, with separate lives

- Their expectations and demands are not your work to fix

- Each person must take responsibility for their own health and wholeness

- Boundaries allow both parties to show up authentically and whole for one another

Stand confidently in your power. Their reactions reflect their own unhealed wounds. You got this.

Learning To Say No

Many raised in traumatic family environments struggle to say no because compliance and obedience felt safest growing up. Exercise your right to say no.

Practice saying "No thank you" to small requests from safe people. Build up to declining more challenging demands from family. Embrace saying no without guilt or excuses.

Your time, energy, attention and life belong fully to you. You do not need permission to make self-honoring choices. Just say no.

Protecting Your Energy

You have the right to protect your energy by limiting contact with relatives who deplete or disturb your peace. You are not required to accept mistreatment or toxicity.

Give yourself permission to:

- Not pick up calls from relatives who disrespect you

- Leave family gatherings that deteriorate into drama or conflict

- Politely decline invitations you resent or exhaust you

Your sensitivity, safety and home are priorities. Even cherished family does not get unlimited access if they abuse privileges.

Prioritizing Self-Care

Make listening to your own needs for restoration as important as showing up for others. You cannot healthfully sustain connections without nurturing yourself first.

Block off daily time for:

- Centering prayer or meditation

- Engaging in physical activities that invigorate you.

- Creative pursuits that enliven your spirit

- Reading or listening to audios that inspire you

- Allowing rest when tired

You deserve to prioritize self-care without shame or guilt. Your worth is never dependent on what you can do for others.

Establishing Safe Family Interactions

Aim for family interactions that are mutually uplifting. Communicate values of respect, understanding and emotional safety. Walk away when violated.

Request relatives:

- Not pressure you about private matters

- Not make negative comments about your life choices

- Share air time in discussions rather than lecturing

- Show interest in your perspective too

Model speaking up about discomfort and listening openly without judging one another. Make kindness the norm.

Letting Go with Love

With some relatives, maintaining healthy boundaries or contact may be impossible, even for the sake of children. In these painful cases, letting go with love can be healthiest.

Grieve what cannot be. Release anger and resentment through prayer, journaling, support groups, or talk therapy. Sending distant love preserves your light.

Honoring Your Wholeness

You are a whole, wise, capable adult outside any inherited narratives or legacies. Your identity resides within, not in external labels, histories, or outdated role definitions. The choice of who you are at this moment is yours.

Set boundaries with compassion for yourself and relatives, while honoring the fullness of your being. Wholeness awaits.

Healing generational trauma requires courageously charting your own course. As you establish healthy new boundaries, both your ancestors and descendants light torches to brighten your way forward.

The next chapter explores the power of forgiveness in releasing intergenerational burdens in order to relate to your lineage from a centered place of peace.

Chapter 11: Forgiveness as a Path to Freedom

Forgiveness is an act of deep spiritual healing that allows us to release pain inherited from ancestors' unresolved wounds and traumas.

This chapter explores:

- Understanding true forgiveness
- How forgiveness heals
- Forgiving yourself
- Forgiving those who caused harm
- Accessing empathy
- Rituals and ceremonies for forgiveness
- Forgiveness as a process
- Learning to forgive situations and systems
- The freedom of letting go
- Reconciliation when possible

Forgiveness does not condone harmful actions. It simply loosens trauma's grip on your psyche so you can relate to your lineage from a centered place of peace.

Understanding True Forgiveness

Many resist forgiveness because they believe it means excusing harm, denying anger or revictimizing trauma survivors.

In truth, forgiveness is about your personal healing, not the perpetrator. It relinquishes justified rage that otherwise keeps you chained to the past. Forgiveness untangles your spirit.

Forgiveness recognizes the humanity in those who harmed you without minimizing the damage done. It acknowledges wrongs in context without hatred. This wisdom enables moving forward.

How Forgiveness Heals

Studies confirm that practicing heart-centered forgiveness physically and psychologically heals trauma's impacts in profound ways by:

- Lessening depression, anxiety, grief, and PTSD

- Reducing inflammation and improving cardiovascular health

- Reducing blood pressure and decreasing stress hormone levels

- Strengthening immune and nervous system function

- Increasing feelings of empowerment, trust, and self-worth

- Promoting perspective-taking and emotional regulation abilities

Forgiveness replenishes mind, body and soul depleted by traumatic burdens. It is an act of self-reclamation.

Forgiving Yourself

Begin by forgiving yourself for any guilt or shame you carry related to your ancestors' trauma and dysfunction.

You did not choose the family or personal wounds inherited. Any coping mechanisms that developed served a purpose at the time. Your existence has deep meaning despite inherited burdens. Release self-judgment.

Forgiving Those Who Caused Harm

The next step is finding empathy for ancestors and living relatives who caused intergenerational harm.

Remember that trauma begets trauma. Hurt people often hurt others unconsciously. Our shared humanity makes us vulnerable to similar missteps under stress and suffering. With awareness, we can interrupt cycles by doing better.

Focus less on what relatives did wrong, and more on the contexts and factors that limited their choices. Trauma survivors deserve both accountability and compassion.

Accessing Empathy

Empathy expands our capacity for forgiveness. Try seeing through the lens of relatives who caused harm:

- How did their own trauma, grief, poverty, oppression or addiction constrain them?

- What inner wounds, insecurities and unmet needs might they have had?

- How did systems and institutions fail them?

- What examples or values shaped their biased belief systems?

- What positive qualities or intentions offset their destructive behaviors?

Understanding where loved ones were coming from emotionally helps us change the narrative from blaming to forgiving.

Rituals and Ceremonies for Forgiveness

Ritual facilitates the spiritual process of forgiveness.

Try lighting candles and speaking prayers of understanding and release for ancestors. Write unsent letters expressing forgiveness. Create art, songs or poems to transmute pain into healing. Share grief with supportive community.

The symbolism of rituals unites intention with action to help move energy stuck in the past.

Forgiveness As a Process

Rarely does forgiveness happen as a single act. More commonly it unfolds in layers, day by day, through an ongoing practice.

When anger or hurt arises again, breathe through it. Avoid dwelling on stories that reinforce wounds without contextualizing the humanity. Stay consistent with forgiveness. Each moment of empathy and compassion builds upon the last.

Learning To Forgive Situations and Systems

In cases of cultural trauma and oppression, forgiveness may also involve releasing hatred toward groups, systems and social conditions that endangered or excluded your ancestors.

This level of forgiveness does not justify injustice. It acknowledges the broader atmosphere of fear or ignorance that breeds bias so we can challenge it consciously. Even systems arise from human frailties and blind spots which we all share. There are always courageous allies within communities who counterbalance injustice. Allow your heart to discern nuance.

The Freedom of Letting Go

Completing the forgiveness process lifts a heavy weight from your psyche and allows you to relate to your lineage from a place of peace.

Stay vigilant of old stories or toxicity that try to hook you backward into pain. Forgiveness releases you to move forward unburdened. What happened in the past becomes meaningful fuel for growth, not baggage.

Reconciliation When Possible

In some situations, forgiveness can open doors to contact, connection and reconciliation with living relatives after estrangement.

Take small risks, maintain healthy boundaries, and expect occasional setbacks. Not all relatives may be open or safe to reunite with. But forgiveness at minimum removes hatred, brings understanding and allows everyone to grow.

Forgiveness is a gift first to yourself - an act of grace that frees your spirit, transforms generational trauma, and reshapes entire family legacies for the better. It creates space for what truly matters most: love.

The next chapter explores mindful communication and emotional intelligence practices to break destructive family patterns and build healthy connections across generations.

Chapter 12: Communicating and Connecting in Healthy Ways

Transforming family legacies shaped by inherited trauma requires learning to communicate and relate to one another in more conscious, vulnerable and emotionally intelligent ways.

This chapter provides strategies to practice:

- Compassionate listening
- Emotion coaching
- Nonviolent communication
- Managing conflict maturely
- Speaking your truth
- Setting discussion agreements
- Relating beyond roles
- Quality time and sharing activities
- Not taking things personally
- Moving from judgement to curiosity
- Giving the gift of presence

By fostering intimacy through mindful communication, you heal ancestral wounds and model healthy bonding for generations to come.

Compassionate Listening

Healing communication starts with listening deeply, attentively and without judgment to understand relatives' perspectives and feelings beneath the surface.

Listen for emotion behind the story. Allow silence for reflection. Ask curious questions to learn more, not debate. Repeat back what you heard. Listening with empathy builds trust and connection.

Emotion Coaching

Emotion coaching is guiding relatives through emotions with empathy so they build confidence in expressing themselves healthfully.

Help distressed family name their feelings. Validate their right to emotions. Set limits on harmful behavior calmly, not punitively. Reframe struggles through a lens of mutual understanding. Your support helps them integrate experiences constructively.

Nonviolent Communication

Nonviolent communication focuses expressing ourselves and listening to others in ways that foster mutual compassion through:

- Observing facts versus evaluating

- Identifying emotions and needs versus criticizing

- Requesting wants respectfully versus demanding

- Expressing appreciation for what you value in others

This approach reduces defensive reactions that derail communication.

Managing Conflict Maturely

Commit to engaging conflict thoughtfully as a means of growth.

Take space to cool down and gain perspective if needed. Share feelings vulnerably. Allow others to vent without absorbing anger. Affirm mutual positive intentions. Brainstorm solutions together.

Peacefully resolving differences deepens trust and maturity.

Speaking Your Truth

Be open about your boundaries, feelings, perspectives and experiences that help relatives understand you better.

Share memories, hopes, spiritual beliefs, personal values, worries, delights and wisdom that widen your shared story. Speaking truthfully about what matters expresses care.

Setting Family Discussion Agreements

Agree on healthy communication ground rules for family discussions such as:

- Giving each person uninterrupted time to share thoughts

- No belittling, shaming or violence

- Active listening without devices or distractions

- Self-monitoring to deescalate rising tensions

- Taking breaks if needed before reconvening

Outlining expectations creates a secure foundation for authentic relating.

Relating Beyond Family Roles

Move beyond limiting assigned family roles and dynamics that inhibit mutually empowering relationships.

Relate to parents as fellow adults. Treat in-laws as chosen family. Develop personal friendships with siblings. See elders' humanity.

Forge a new extended family through bonds of affinity rather than obligation.

Quality Time and Shared Activities

The simple act of giving focused attention and enjoying activities together counteracts trauma's legacy of disconnection.

Share meals, games, sports, projects, trips, rituals and interests that provide opportunities for laughter, teamwork, physical affection and making happy memories. Uplifting shared experiences are the building blocks of healthy relationships.

Not Taking Things Personally

When relatives act out their own inner wounds through criticism, disappointment or even rejection - try not to take it personally. Their reactions likely reflect inherited insecurities more than your worth.

Maintain compassion for their internal struggles. You cannot control their triggers or growth process. Hold on to your truth.

Moving From Judgment to Curiosity

Catch yourself making assumptions and instead get curious. Ask relatives questions to better understand their motives and contexts.

Suspend accusations. Imagine reasons they may have made choices you disagree with. Look for common ground. Curiosity transforms judgment into insight.

Giving the Gift of Presence

The most precious gift you can offer family is sincere presence - putting devices down, sharing your true self, and making each person feel heard, appreciated and valued.

Presence heals through little moments - a hug, listening patiently, cheering successes, comforting in grief, laughing at jokes, appreciating quirks. It reassures that we are not alone.

Healing generational trauma transforms how we relate at fundamental levels - from separation to intimate connection, from fear to trust, from roles to authenticity, from toxicity to mutual care.

In giving and receiving love fully, we write the next chapter together.

The following chapter explores how to raise conscious, empowered and emotionally intelligent children able to rewrite ancestral narratives positively.

Chapter 13: Raising the Next Generation Consciously

As you heal from inherited family trauma, you have the profound opportunity to spare your own children from unconsciously repeating painful generational cycles.

This chapter provides guidance on:

- Breaking destructive parenting patterns

- Fostering secure attachment

- Modeling emotional intelligence

- Cultivating child self-esteem

- Teaching resilience and growth mindset

- Exploring family history together

- Disciplining without shame

- Supporting diverse identities

- Encouraging healthy boundaries

- Nurturing gifts and passions

- Letting go with love and trust

- Healing your inner child

- Empowering your lineage

Mindful parenting focused on connection, communication, empowerment and healing transforms generational trauma so that your children and grandchildren may thrive.

Breaking Destructive Parenting Patterns

Commit to showing up consciously and avoiding unconscious repetition of relatives' harmful parenting choices that wounded you:

- Verbal abuse, criticism, possessiveness
- Physical discipline or aggression
- Emotional neglect and detachment
- Manipulation, coercion or control
- Enmeshment and lack of boundaries
- Conditional approval based on achievement

Your family's pain ends with you. Make the pledge to parent with wisdom, patience and compassion.

Fostering Secure Attachment

Prioritize building a secure emotional attachment with your child through:

- Attuning to their needs, emotions, hopes and fears
- Physical affection and verbal affirmation
- Soothing and comforting distress
- Protecting them consistently
- Celebrating milestones and victories
- Admitting mistakes and apologizing
- Respecting their unique personality and voice

Secure attachment results from dependable nurturing. Show up.

Modeling Emotional Intelligence

Demonstrate managing emotions effectively through challenging experiences.

- Label your own feelings appropriately

- Express anger calmly without blaming

- Be transparent when disappointed but not vindictive

- Apologize for overreactions after cooling down

- Show resilience and optimism when faced with problems

Kids imitate parents' emotional regulation skills. Your examples will guide them for life.

Cultivating Child Self-Esteem

Counteract ancestral shame and silence negative self-talk by nurturing their self-worth:

- Affirm their talents, efforts and character frequently

- Avoid criticism and comparison with others

- Allow them to make age-appropriate choices

- Ask their opinions and encourage input

- Support their interests and dreams unconditionally

- Collaborate rather than dictate

When children feel valued intrinsically, they internalize secure self-regard.

Teaching Resilience and Growth Mindset

Build children's ability to bounce back from challenges and see failures as learning opportunities:

- Help themsetLabel emotions/frustrations

- Praise effort over innate talent

- Celebrate perseverance and courage

- Allow natural consequences instead of rescuing

- Encourage problem-solving before intervening

- Model optimism, gratitude, and humor during trials

Developing resilience prevents inherited helplessness. Your faith in them teaches them faith in themselves.

Exploring Family History Together

Share details about your family history at age-appropriate times. Invite their questions.

Discuss ancestors' places of origin, migrations/ displacements, livelihoods, and values. Share family triumphs and challenges. Teach the importance of kindness.

Understanding their roots helps ground kids with a sense of heritage and shared humanity beyond themselves. Learn together.

Disciplining Without Shame

Set firm limits on behavior while making clear the child is inherently worthy, not rotten:

- Establish consistent boundaries and expectations

- Remain calm when reinforcing rules

- Avoid cruel/excessive punishments

- Focus discipline on values, not compliance

- Model taking accountability without self-hate

- Give opportunities to make amends and learn

"Discipline" means to teach. Rules anchored in mutual respect allow children to internalize self-control.

Supporting Diverse Identities

Provide safety for your child to explore their authentic gender identity, sexual orientation, neurodiversity, religious perspectives, etc.

Never force them to conform to biases. Celebrate their journey of self-discovery. Stand up against bigotry and oppression. Foster diverse community.

When children feel loved unconditionally, they bloom into their fullest selves without self-rejection.

Encouraging Healthy Boundaries

Equip children to set physical, emotional and intellectual boundaries:

- Teach them to say no to unwanted touch/demands

- Do not force physical affection, food or activities

- Respect their right to have secrets and private time

- Step back to allow age-appropriate risk-taking

- Trust their unfolding process

Boundaries foster self-awareness, confidence, and autonomy - preventing compliance and victimization.

Nurturing Gifts and Passions

Provide opportunities to discover their innate gifts outside inherited family roles and limitations:

- Expose them to diverse experiences

- Encourage any interests that call to them

- Prioritize creativity and free play

- Allow time outdoors and in nature

- Embrace their quirks and originality

- Resist rushing structured activities before self-discovery

When children follow their inner spark, they light the way for future generations.

Letting Go with Love and Trust

When the time comes, trust you have equipped your children to craft their own lives and relationships.

Release fears for their path ahead. Have faith in seeds of emotional intelligence, resilience, morality and wisdom planted. They carry your loving imprint within their spirit always.

Your job is to let go and allow their story to unfold.

Healing Your Inner Child

Address your own unmet childhood needs through loving your kids' free and vulnerable spirit. Receive the nurturance you longed for vicariously.

Play, wonder, cry, hope and dream alongside them. Imagine parenting little you. Fulfill the wishes of your wounded inner child through the healing gift of mindful parenting.

Empowering Your Lineage

With consistent love, emotional availability, modeling, teaching, forgiving, and letting go, you transform ancestral trauma into empowerment for generations to come.

The greatest inheritance you can offer your descendents is breaking unhealthy cycles and knowing their worth. By healing your lineage, their future is bright with potential.

Your conscious parenting ripples outward through generations, rewriting your family's story from pain to promise. Every loving choice matters.

The concluding chapter will summarize key lessons from our journey of understanding and healing inherited family trauma so you may move forward with hope and confidence on your path ahead.

Conclusion: Breaking Free and Moving Forward

Our journey of exploring inherited family trauma comes to a close, but your journey is only beginning. This conclusion summarizes key lessons to integrate so you may move forward with hope:

You Are Not Alone

If you carry the burden of unresolved ancestral wounds, you are not alone. Many struggles with the lingering impacts of intergenerational trauma passed down unconsciously.

Your experiences echo through communities and families everywhere. Have compassion for yourself and others traveling this path with you. Together transformation unfolds.

It Is Possible to Heal

While inherited trauma shapes much of your inner world, healing is absolutely possible. By better understanding the past and releasing old wounds through grief, embodiment practices, counseling, ritual, bonding, and forgiveness you alter family legacies.

Generational trauma is painful but does not have to be permanent. You have the power to change your ancestral line.

The Past Does Not Define You

Although you inherited certain traumas, tendencies and burdens from ancestors, they do not dictate your future. Their stories shape but do not define you.

You get to consciously choose new patterns and projections. You are not doomed - you get to rewrite the next chapter. Your life belongs to you.

Relationships are Key

Trauma isolates, so communal healing is vital. Sharing your family history and inner process with supportive loved ones allows their care to transform your nervous system and narratives.

You liberate something in one another. Bonds robust enough to hold your shadows without judgment restore wholeness. The journey was never meant to be traversed alone.

Embrace Emotions as Messengers

Suppressed emotions like anger, grief and fear become toxic over time. Allow yourself to fully feel and express any surfacing feelings as part of your lineage's healing process.

Your "negative" emotions have important wisdom to share if you listen without judgement. They guide you toward integration and greater self-awareness.

Trauma Can Make Sense in Context

Terrible ancestral events and dysfunctional family patterns can finally make sense when illuminated in their proper historical context and social realities.

Compassion arises when you comprehend the conditions that bred behaviors like abuse, addiction, abandonment, emotional unavailability and authoritarianism. By contextualizing, you depersonalize inherited burdens.

Forgiveness Transforms the Meaning of Trauma

With understanding comes forgiveness. Despite justified anger about past harms, forgiving those who perpetuated generational trauma positions you to move forward in strength, not victimhood.

Forgiveness alters the meaning of trauma from something senseless into something used for growth. It allows you to shape your life's message.

You Become An Agent of Healing

Inherited trauma ends with you. By doing your own work to process old wounds, establish healthy boundaries, cultivate mindfulness, grieve, embrace vulnerability and relate consciously, you prevent perpetuating past pain.

You can be the ancestor your descendants look back upon with pride and gratitude for transforming the family systems. Your consciousness impacts generations.

It Takes Time and Patience

Healing from inherited family trauma is ongoing, not one decision. Emotions and revelations surface gradually in stages when you create internal safety to accept them.

Some days you will feel strong, other days confused or despairing. Like peeling an onion, be patient with the process of working through generations of pain. Keep going.

Your Story Weaves into A Larger Story

Your family lineage and generational trauma exist within a larger web of human experiences. Find perspective by situating your story within the shared human quest to make meaning of suffering and pass lessons on to future generations.

You are one chapter in an age-old storyline. Your personal growth ripples outward.

Love Carried the Past, Love Will Heal the Future

For all the pain passed down through your family history, love passed down as well - resiliency, devotion, courage, commitment, kindness, hope.

Reconnect to the power of love as the force that kept your ancestors surviving and dreaming of better days for their descendants. Love will heal your lineage just as it gave their lives meaning. Love always remains.

The journey of healing inherited family trauma will challenge you, change you, and ultimately empower you. By releasing old wounds, you make space for whatever is waiting to be born in and through you.

You honor the past by learning its lessons, without allowing the past to own you. Keep choosing growth and life. Your ancestors' spirits guide you, your descendants need you, and you owe it to yourself to walk proudly into your fullest expression.

This is the work of generations. Your future begins now.

About the Author.

Dr. Monday Farouq is an esteemed psychologist and trauma healing guide who has dedicated his life's work to understanding and transforming inherited family trauma.

With over 15 years of experience as a therapist, researcher, and author, Dr. Farouq's pioneering insights into intergenerational healing have touched countless lives. His compassionate approach is grounded in the belief that we all carry ancestral wounds, and that those wounds can be healed with the right support and guidance.

In his psychotherapy practice, Dr. Farouq helps individuals gently unravel the threads connecting their struggles to the unresolved grief, loss, abuse, adversity, and dysfunction carried through generations of their family. By shining light on these patterns in a spirit of understanding rather than blame, he empowers people to process old pain, rewrite negative cycles, and step forward as authors of their own lives.

Dr. Farouq's expertise derives not only from his training in psychology and trauma recovery, but his personal experiences navigating family challenges and honoring his complex cultural heritage. This fuels his ability to hold space for clients' diverse stories with humility, patience and profound heart.

His book "Breaking Free from Inherited Family Trauma", is a roadmap to transform generational suffering into generational strength.

Dr. Monday Farouq is married with kids, and currently resides in Lagos, Nigeria.